AF439559

WHO WON IN THE RACE FOR SPACE?

History Book Grade 6
Children's History

Speedy Publishing LLC

40 E. Main St. #1156

Newark, DE 19711

www.speedypublishing.com

Copyright 2017

In this book, we're going to talk about who won the Race for Space. So, let's get right to it!

THE BEGINNING OF THE COLD WAR

After World War II came to a close in 1945, the relationship between the Soviet Union and the democracies of the West began to change. The Soviet Union had been on the side of the Allied Powers in World War II and had fought with the United States and other members of the Allied Powers against Hitler's Germany.

COLD
WAR

However, after the war was over, the Western democracies began to mistrust the communist Soviets. The United States and other democratic countries didn't want communism to spread to other countries of the world.

They were also very concerned about the brutal dictator, Joseph Stalin, who was the leader of the Soviet Union at that time. This period of tension between the Soviets and the United States was known as the Cold War and continued until the Soviet Union collapsed in 1991.

JOSEPH STALIN

THE FIVE CREW MEMBERS OF ASTP SITTING AROUND
A MINIATURE MODEL OF THEIR SPACECRAFT
STAFFORD
NASA
SLAYTON
NASA
BRAND
NASA

The tension between these world powers came out in three different ways:

- Proxy Wars

- The Arms Race

- The Space Race

PROXY WARS

Sometimes a war would break out between two countries, such as North Korea and South Korea. The Soviets backed North Korea and the United States backed South Korea. Even though the two superpowers weren't fighting each other directly, they were still fighting each other indirectly. A number of these types of wars took place.

SOUTH KOREA VS NORTH KOREA

ARMS RACE: ANNUAL BASE WEAPONS LOAD
EGLIN AIR FORCE BASE

THE ARMS RACE

The other way that the United States and the Soviet Union fought each other indirectly was the Arms Race. Each of them tried to obtain the best and largest weapons, such as nuclear bombs. The idea was that if each side had an equivalent amount of dangerous power then they would be evenly matched, so it would stop them from attacking each other.

THE SPACE RACE

Each power wanted to demonstrate that it had the best scientists, the best technology, and the best rockets. They were each trying to accomplish certain space missions first, such as putting a spacecraft with an astronaut in orbit and landing astronauts on the moon. This competition became known as the Space Race.

SOVIET SPACE PROGRAM

THE RACE BEGINS IN EARNEST

The leaders in the United States and the leaders in the Soviet Union both realized how critical rocket technology was becoming to their opportunity for military dominance. They each wanted to have the superior rockets.

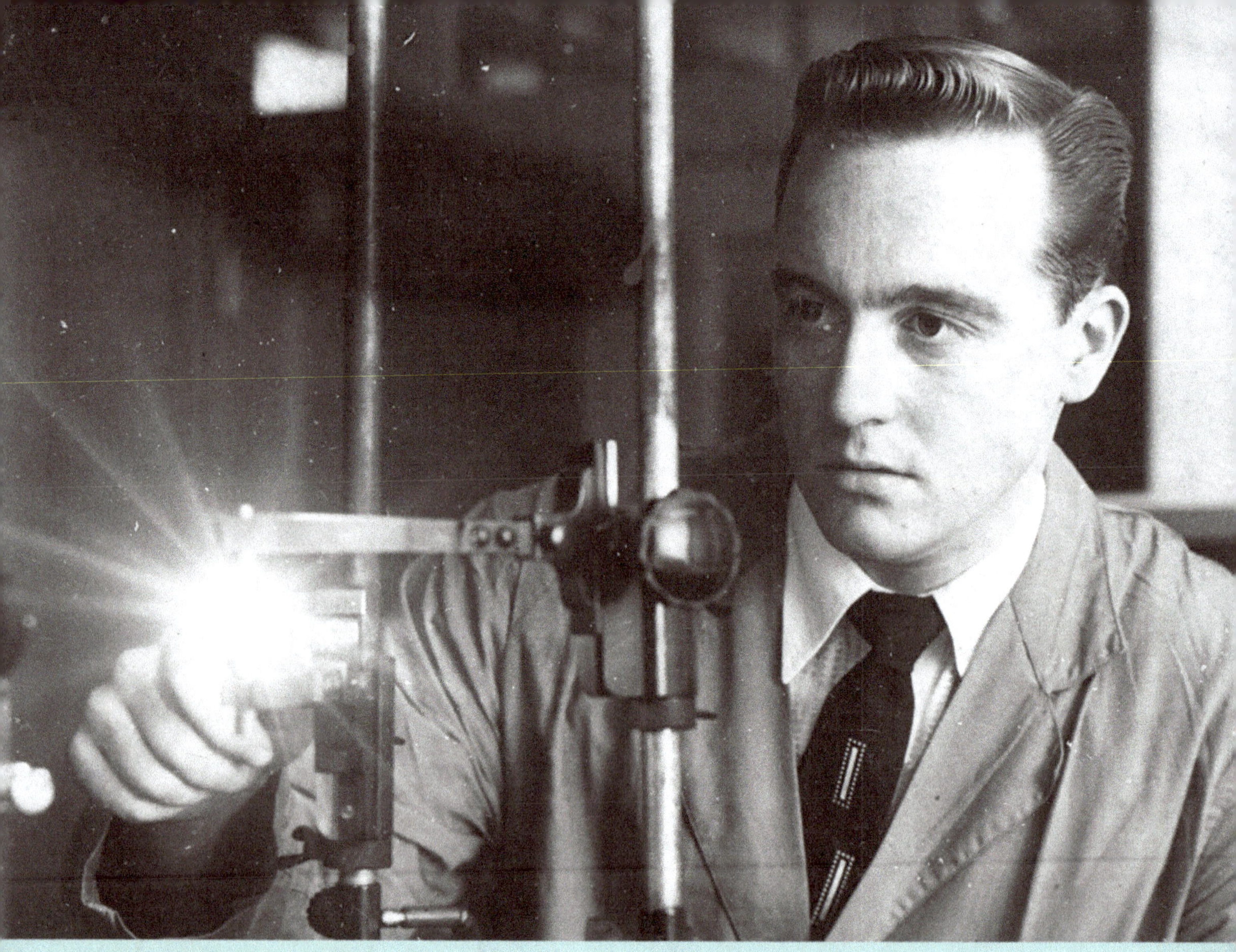

Ironically, both sides hired scientists from Germany, their former enemy in World War II.

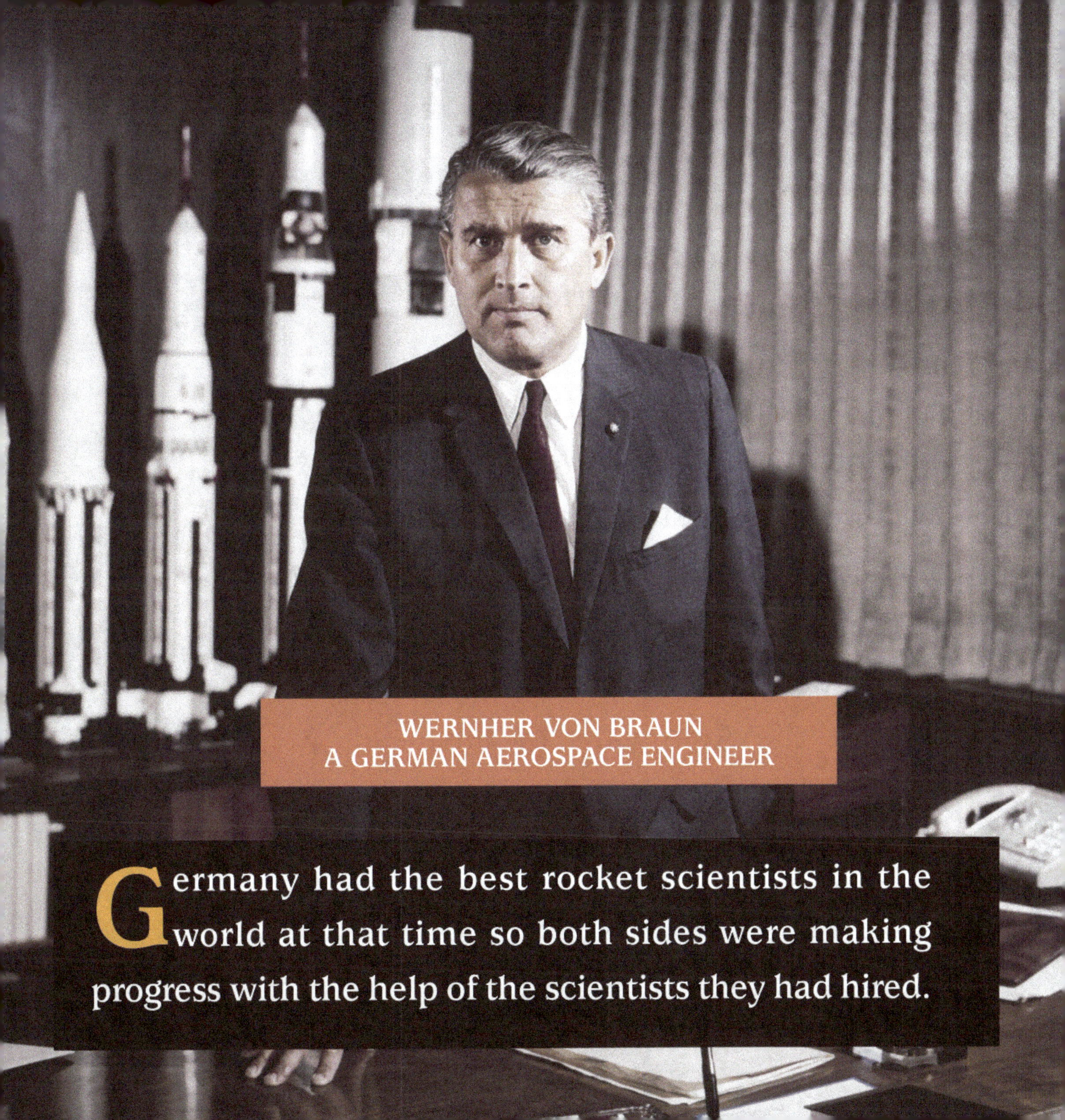

Germany had the best rocket scientists in the world at that time so both sides were making progress with the help of the scientists they had hired.

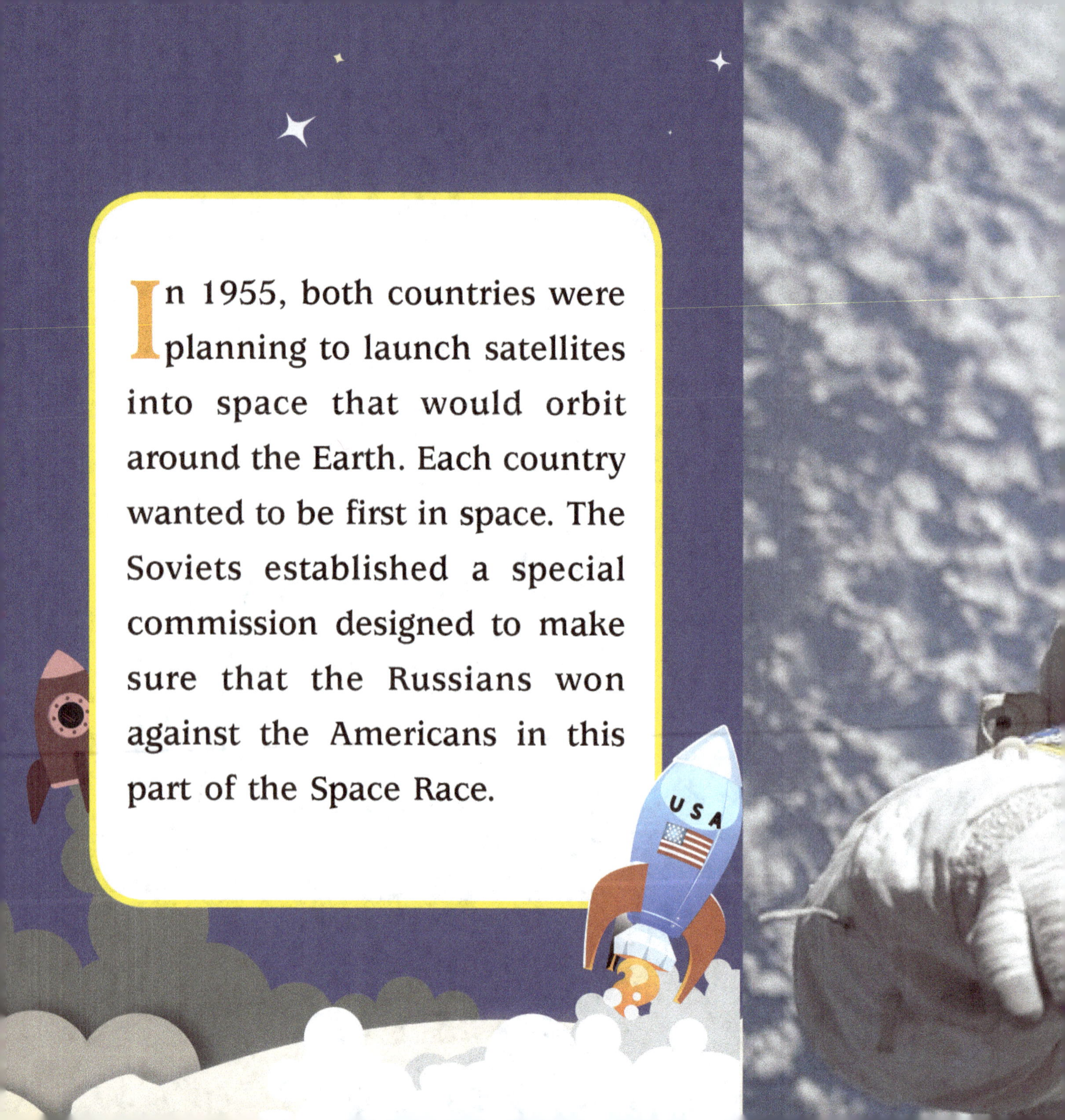

In 1955, both countries were planning to launch satellites into space that would orbit around the Earth. Each country wanted to be first in space. The Soviets established a special commission designed to make sure that the Russians won against the Americans in this part of the Space Race.

A COSMONAUT IN SPACE

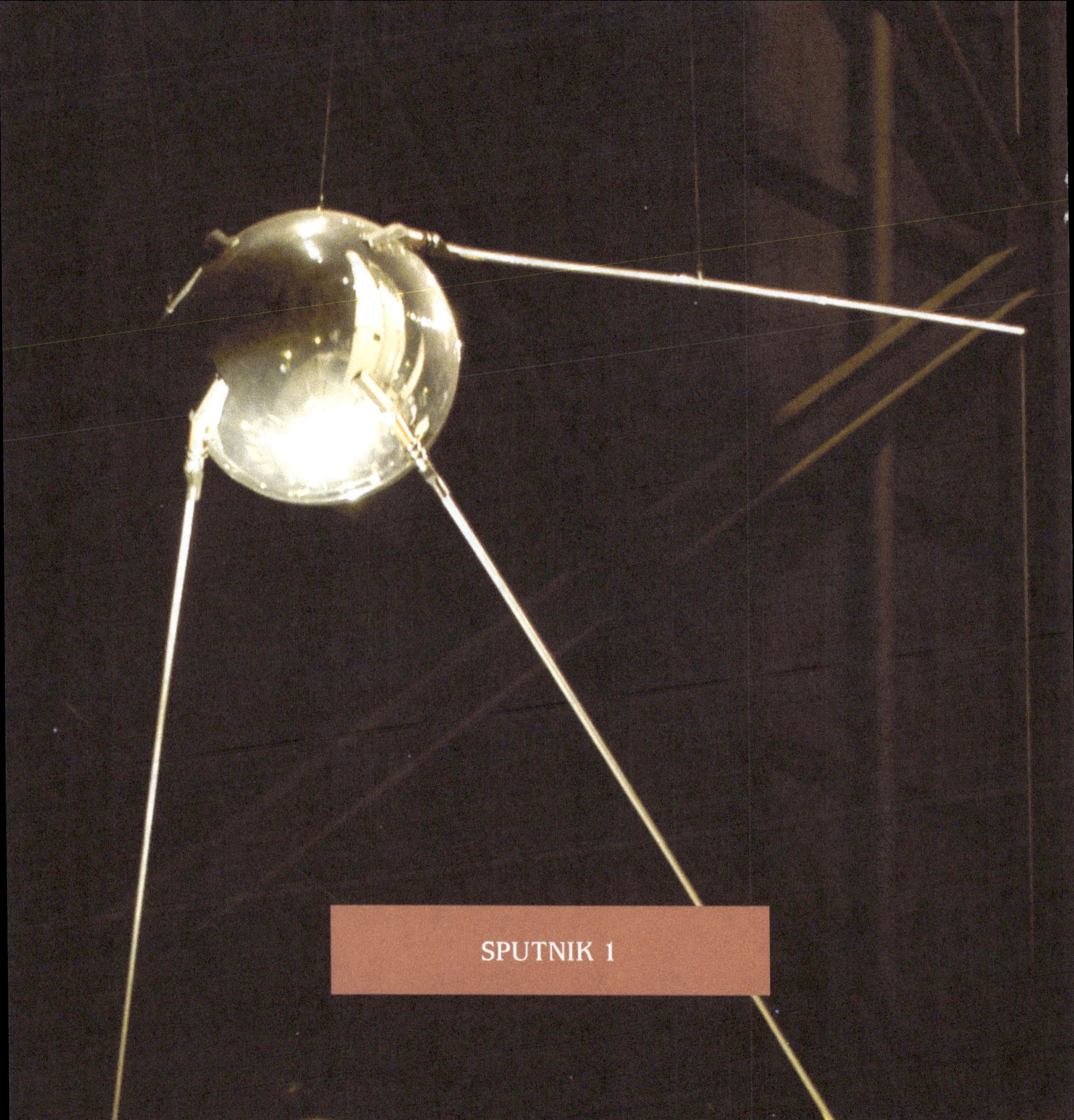
SPUTNIK 1

The Soviet Union was very proud when they were able to get the first satellite up in space on the 4th of October 1957. Their new satellite was called Sputnik I. They had taken the lead in the race and leaders in the United States weren't pleased. Four months later, the United States launched its first successful satellite called Explorer I.

THE FIRST MAN IN SPACE

The Soviets were working hard in their rocket laboratories. They wanted to be the first to put a man into space. On the 12th of April in 1961, cosmonaut Yuri Gagarin became the very first man in space. He orbited the Earth in the Russian spacecraft called Vostok I.

YURI GAGARIN

ALAN SHEPARD, COMMANDER OF APOLLO 14

The United States launched their rocket, the Freedom 7, three weeks after the Russians. Astronaut Alan Shepard was on board. However, the Freedom 7 wasn't put into an orbit around the Earth. The first United States orbiting spacecraft was the Friendship 7, which was put into orbit on the 20th of February in 1962 with astronaut John Glenn on board.

THE RACE TO THE MOON

The Americans were humiliated now that the Soviets were so far ahead on their space travels. President John F. Kennedy made what became a famous announcement to Congress. He wanted the United States to be the first country to land a man on the moon. He told Congress that he felt it was critical for an American astronaut to be the first to set foot on the moon. Congress agreed and the Apollo program was started.

JOHN F. KENNEDY

GEMINI 6 7

THE GEMINI PROGRAM

At the same time that the Apollo program was going on, the United States also started the Gemini program. Its mission was to develop and refine the technology for use on the spacecraft that the Apollo astronauts would be launching.

The Gemini program embarked on numerous important research projects:

- Scientists learned how to adjust a spacecraft's orbit.
- Astronauts spent time in orbit so scientists could learn about the effects of zero gravity on the human body.
- Two spacecraft were joined together in space.
- Astronauts walked outside the spacecraft on their first "space walks."

ASTRONAUT OUTSIDE
THE SPACECRAFT

ASTRONAUT BUZZ ALDRIN, LUNAR MODULE
PILOT OF THE FIRST LUNAR LANDING MISSION

THE FIRST MAN ON THE MOON

After years of test flights and intense training, three American astronauts were ready to go to the moon. The Apollo 11 was sent up into space on the 16th of July in 1969. The crew was made up of:

- Neil Armstrong, who was the Commander
- Buzz Aldrin, who was the Lunar Module pilot
- Michael Collins, who was the Command Module pilot

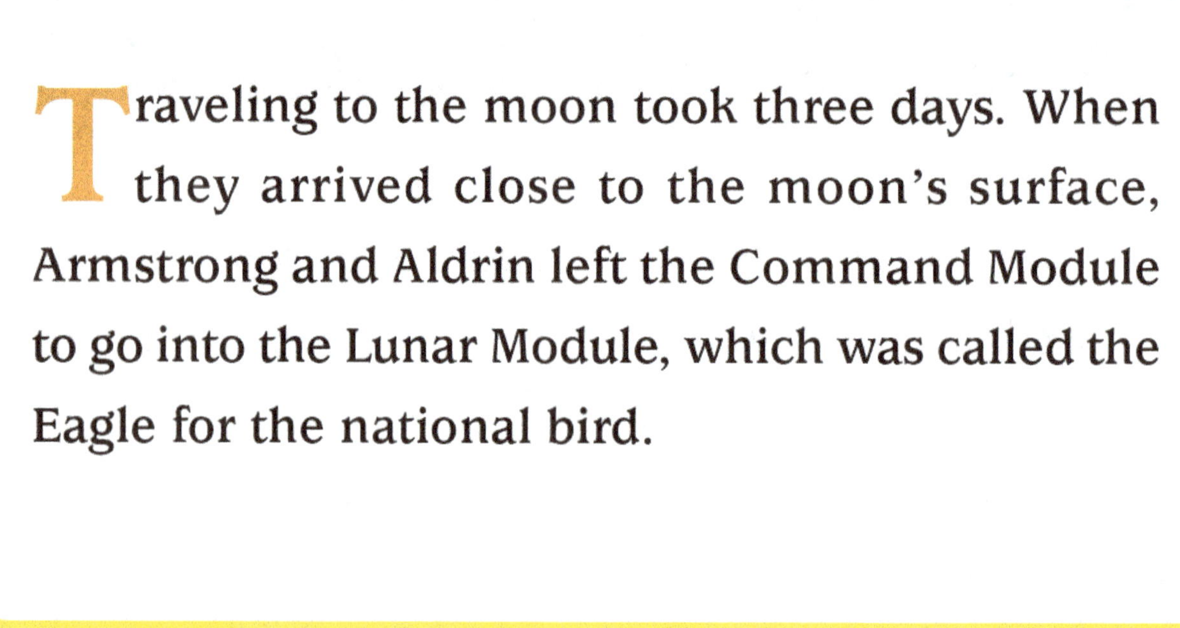

Traveling to the moon took three days. When they arrived close to the moon's surface, Armstrong and Aldrin left the Command Module to go into the Lunar Module, which was called the Eagle for the national bird.

THE APOLLO 11 PRIME CREW

Michael Collins stayed in the Command Module and was in orbit around the moon for a full day before his fellow astronauts rejoined him.

There were some glitches at the last minute and Armstrong had to manually land the Lunar Module.

When the Lunar Module had safely landed, Armstrong sent a communication to the scientists back on Earth to tell them "the Eagle has landed." It was the 20th of July in 1969—a day that would be one of the most important in human history.

MOON LANDING, APOLLO 11

Neil Armstrong went down the ladder of the Eagle and carefully placed his first step on the moon as he said the now-famous line "That's one small step for man," and then he continued, "one giant leap for mankind."

The world was watching on television and when the astronauts came back they were hailed as heroes with a ticker-tape parade in New York City. It was an exciting time!

WHEN DID THE SPACE RACE END?

Thanks to the successful landing of astronauts on the moon, the United States was now ahead in the Space Race. Six years later another historic event took place when the first joint mission of the Americans and the Soviets happened.

It was called the Apollo-Soyez project. Although the Cold War wouldn't end for another sixteen years, the race for the domination of space had come to an end.

ASTRONAUT AND COSMONAUT SPACESUITS

FASCINATING FACTS ABOUT THE SPACE RACE

The Soviets called their rocket pilots cosmonauts, which essentially means "the sailors of the cosmos."

The Americans called their rocket pilots astronauts, which essentially means "the sailors of the stars."

The root word for both cosmonauts and astronauts comes from the Greek word, "nautes," which means "sailor."

Before President John F. Kennedy was assassinated in 1963, the Soviet Union and the United States were entertaining the idea of working together to land a man on the lunar surface. However, after Kennedy was killed, the Russians decided not to pursue working with the Americans.

The Detroit News EXTRA

KENNEDY DEAD

Slain in Car by Dallas Assassin

Romney Indicates Doubts About Backing Goldwater

(Related Story on Page 1C)

By GLENN ENGLE
Detroit News Political Writer

OMAHA, Nov. 22 —Michigan's Gov. Romney said today that he has reservations about the views of Arizona Senator Barry Goldwater on three major issues.

Pressed by reporters covering the Midwestern Governors' Conference, Romney singled out "three areas of concern" over Goldwater's views:

- Excessive power in the hands of big industry and big labor.
- Right-to-work laws.
- Civil rights.

Goldwater, he said, "seems to be worried about excess power in the hands of labor but not in the hands of employers."

OPPOSED UNION CURB

Romney has spoken out repeatedly against right-to-work laws, which would bar unions from forcing employers to join as a condition of employment. Goldwater once led a national drive for right-to-work legislation but since has backed away from his position.

On civil rights, Romney has favored free access to public accommodations for all. Goldwater has advocated that this issue be left to individual states.

As for Goldwater's leading rival, Nelson A. Rockefeller, Romney refused to comment on the New York governor's recent divorce and remarriage other than that "the people will express themselves on that."

DIFFERS ON TVA, TOO

Ford Buys Lions; Fight Threatened

By KEN DUNN

Stockholders today approved the sale of the Detroit Lions to William Clay Ford for six million dollars.

Board Asks Talks With Teachers

By HARRY SALSINGER
Detroit News Education Writer

Despite what it called a legal question on collective bargaining for teachers, the Detroit Board of Education has offered to discuss the problems of a collective bargaining election with teacher representatives.

Trooper Halted, Released

Was Stopped by Police as He Fled Bank Raid

(Related Stories on Page 1C)

By JOSEPH E. WOLFF
Of Our Pontiac Bureau

A State Police trooper was in jail today for a bungled bank robbery — after having been stopped, questioned as a possible suspect, then released by two suburban officers while he was at the wheel of the getaway car.

"I wish I could tell you why I did it," Trooper Andy Salkovich was quoted as telling his superiors. "But I can't.

"I just don't know why I was driving by the bank when I got the idea."

Almost at pistol point early today were Patrolmen Charles Doner and Ralph Bachorski of the Waterford Township Police.

DWIGHT D. EISENHOWER

The United States might have had the very first orbiting satellite had they been able to use military rockets from the beginning. However, President Eisenhower was concerned that countries around the world would see that as a war threat, so he wanted the United States to launch research rockets.

There were many devastating failures on both sides during the Space Race. There were crashes, close calls, and explosions that caused the death of spacecraft pilots.

SUMMARY

The Cold War began in 1945 when tensions began to rise between the communist Soviet Union and the democratic United States. There were proxy wars where the two superpowers fought each other through conflicts that were happening between two other countries like North and South Korea.

SYMBOL OF COLD WAR

The Arms Race was escalating as the two countries stockpiled dangerous weapons, such as nuclear bombs. In addition, the Russians and Americans wanted to be the first in what

became known as the Space Race. Both countries enlisted the help of German rocket scientists in their quest to be first and win the race.

The Russians had the first satellite and the first orbiting satellite. Inspired by President Kennedy, the Americans went forward to win the race for the first man on the moon. Astronaut Neil Armstrong was the first man to set foot on the moon.

NEIL ARMSTRONG
ARMSTRONG
NASA

USSR
USA
SPACE
RACE

Awesome! Now that you know more about the Race for Space you may want to find out more information about the moon in the Baby Professor book The Faces, Err Phases, of the Moon - Astronomy Book for Kids.

Visit

www.BabyProfessorBooks.com

to download Free Baby Professor eBooks
and view our catalog of new and exciting
Children's Books